G000088539

Watering my Soul

Watering my Soul

Ella Kate Reeves

INNERLIGHT
PUBLISHING

Inner Light Publishing books may be ordered through booksellers or by contacting:

Inner Light Publishing
Innerlightpublish.com
innerlightpublishing@gmail.com

Because of the dynamic nature of the Internet, any web addresses or links contained in this book may have changed since publication and may no longer be valid. The views expressed in this work are solely those of the author and do not necessarily reflect the views of the publisher and the publisher hereby disclaims any responsibility for them.

The author of this book does not dispense medical advice or prescribe the use of any technique as a form of treatment for physical, emotional, or medical problems without the advice of a physician, either directly or indirectly. The intent of the author is only to offer information of a general nature to help you in your quest for emotional and spiritual well-being. In the event you use any of the information in this book for yourself, which is your constitutional right, the author and the publisher assume no responsibility for your actions.

ISBN: 978-0-9923940-1-1 (sc)
ISBN: 978-0-9923940-6-6 (e)

Dedication

There are so many people and experiences to thank for
this book of poetry. So many moments of agony,
mundanity and ecstasy that honour the grief as much as
the expansive experiences.
I would, however, like to mention a few, particular people
who have played such significance in supporting my
writing and poetry:

I dedicate this book to Jamie, a dear friend, writer and
poet, who sadly died in a motorcycle accident when I was
30. He loved my poems as much as my singing voice and
endlessly encouraged me. I also want to thank my Mum,
who has a passion for poetry and my son Louis. Louis has
Friedreich's Ataxia, a rare, degenerative and life
shortening disease and lives with me at home in Brighton
(UK). From the moment of conception, he has endlessly
taught me about what is important in life and
strengthened my soul and spirit, in a way I had never
known possible. I want to thank Seamus, my husband,
for holding me so beautifully and embracing my life (and
writing). I would also like Chris who came with me on
the day of brain surgery and whose poetry inspired me to
put pen to paper in intensive care and ever since.

Contents

INTRODUCTION

Writing is in my family: my Grandpa was a journalist and Mum enjoys writing. I guess I had a 'normal-ish' childhood....whatever 'normal ' means! Dad was an accountant, Mum a psychotherapist and my half sister was 12 years older, so away most of the time. However, Dad is mildly autistic and Mum extremely 'right brained' and also a sannyasin (a follower of Osho Shree Rajneesh). They divorced when I was seven and I lived with my Mum, who had a private psychotherapy practice and worked from home. I saw Dad at weekends and had lots of friends and happy times as a young child. However, I did experience some sexual abuse from a dance teacher which affected me quite deeply, but wasn't able to speak out as I was so young at the time and didn't really understand what was happening or how to speak out, about it.

Things got trickier in my teens and later. I lost friends in accidents, suffered from compulsive overeating and later anorexia nervosa. I was in rehab at 17. I did get into recovery though and went on to get a degree in Media and Cultural Studies and specialised in Shamanic consciousness, contemporary sexual politics and entertainment law. I also had many wild adventures internally and externally until I fell pregnant aged 22.

Louis was born three months prematurely. I had pre-eclampsia and the h.e.l.l.p syndrome. I died for a few minutes after his emergency C-section and that really was a life changing event. Then, when he was aged 4, Louis began to fall a lot. He had been sick quite frequently as a child and never liked walking, nor showed any interest in learning to ride a bike. I never expected the diagnosis "Friedreich's Ataxia".

I have always loved poetry. However, as a kid, I really struggled with dyslexia and found reading books tough. But poetry made more sense to me. It was rhythmic and somehow able to express its own linguistic limitations. I liked that. It had my full attention. I only wrote a couple of poems as a kid (included in this book 'Figgy' and 'Rugu Man'). This was partly because I fell in love with dance when I was 4 and couldn't get enough of it - when I wasn't at school; I was either on stage or in a studio practising.

Dance continued to shape my life and I went on to train to a professional standard and then as a dance and movement therapist and later a psychotherapist and yoga teacher. But, at the same time, my dyslexia made me shy with words and impacted my self-esteem. I was scared to write, as if it just wasn't my 'medium'.

When I fell ill in 2011 and needed brain surgery, it was a shock. I was a single mum caring for a severely disabled son and I needed my body to care for him. It was also high risk surgery and I didn't have much time between diagnosis and surgery to process or come to terms with it.

However, I believe the human spirit is one of the most striking realizations of wildness: it is as beautiful as an ice crystal, as liquidly life-generous as water, as inspired as air. Kernelled up within us all, an intimate wildness, sweet as a nut; a creative drive that simply needs watering - one person's poison is another's medicine and mine had been dance, nature, yoga....and now I needed some way to harness, release and express what I saw, felt and who I was 'becoming'.

I believe many of us in western culture know we are sick. The sick body lacks certain minerals and vitamins and searches for foods containing them. Often, our confused and toxic brain chemistry and pent up emotions lead us to consume all the wrong things. As the body, so the soul.

A handful of times in my life I have felt an absolute demand to go to a specific place or to know and journey with a specific person. I think we often mix up what's medicine and what's poison for the soul and body. I certainly know I have. But, after surgery, I wanted medicine for my sore soul that needed reconnecting to my body and the world as whole.

Being in pain, unable to move and on tons of strong medications following a five hour surgery left me shattered and low. Depression is a wasteland of its own - the psyche, hurt badly enough, will withdraw and won't come back easily or, for some, at all. Like a plant without sap, the body is without dynamism, flair or potency and the psyche wanders far away, lost and lonely. I didn't want to give up - my son needed me to recover and heal. I wanted to give birth to a new version of myself and find some expression, some freedom again.

We all need soul retrieval at various points in our lives and poetry was and still is medicine for my soul."

Ella Kate Reeves

FIGGY

Figgy was a jumping frog
That sprang around a muddy bog
'Spring, Sprong' as he hopped around
Always making an urping' sound
Alas, one day Figgy ran away
And did not come back for many a day.
He wanted to travel the world to explore,
But wasn't really sure what he was searching for.
Then one day Figgy couldn't spring anymore.
He hopped till he dropped and fell to the floor.
As he lay there he felt and finally found
The thing he sought all along – the ground

(Age 9)

RUGU MAN

He will not do what I want him to
Ozzy Guru with a pot belly
"Rugu man am I" he's laughing now
And as he burps I can see broccoli stuck in his silver filling.
This Rugu is no more than me, a man.

I watch the ones who engage him with dedication like
Buddha or even Jesus Christ
They want answers

I like his hairy legs,
His deep blue Levi's that cling to his sturdy thighs
He's a pig, an insecure decadent character, a player.
He'll love me and laugh at me,
He can't break me, deface me, make me.

He orders cognac at the little French café.

Farts out loud and says "Fuck" a lot.

Heaven and Hell is the man who lays at rest and shouts out loud "I AM AWAKE"
Who cares for the question "Is he Fake?"
He's sitting here next to me and we are laughing

(Age 16)

AN OSHO KID'S WISH LIST

So glad you're wearing Orange
and wearin' no bra, Ma.
So glad 'cos you're smiling,
you're alive in it, you're shining!
God knows what you've done
but that "Santa Claus man" on the toilet wall is when it all began
This Osho guy seems to be the key
to this "new diverse liberty" in front of me...
that you've embraced so wholeheartedly
and although the jabba in my house
is way beyond my comprehension and attention
I know you're doing something important, that's clear
So keep going for it, mother dear....
I'm only 7, so guys I don't know, how I feel?
Or why Mums wearing a Mala and divorcin' my Pa!
--- their marriage was always completely surreal...Guess he was a little dead, closed
off...

but I loved him all the same and now my home's an Osho Ashram
for anyone with a Sannyas name!

I want ham sandwiches without crusts, to come home to something familiar with
trust.
I'd like a picket fence and maybe just a little more pretense,
Some stability, familiarity to contain this entire girl's vulnerability...
Not dynamic meditation, primal screams and a variety of ANIMA-LITY!
Now I know you Sannyas bunch ain't bad, sad or mad...
You're beautiful, musical and maybe a tad delusional... but warm transgressional
tribsters — weird and unusual!
Guess y'all on a spiritual, sexual mission
— to transgress your historical emission
But I'm 7 and a GIRL
don't wanna get naked and express.
I wanna sing and twirl!!!!

This girl needs rules and structure...
some conventional grasp of hierarchal pasture.
I love you, Mum...I do
but this is scary... that's just the truth.
I'm a 7-year-old girl lost in a world
of "Kundalini release and orange clothes"
to "always say YES and never withhold"

to surrender to everything...let go and grow!
despite my innate "childish shyness and fear"
and tendency to cut off and disappear...
just another Osho Kid
with a wish list, mother dear.

STRIPPED IT ALL AWAY

A shining seven-year-old dancing star
Sparkling, smiling, bursting with life
A sweet cocktail of energy and innocence
You were thirsty and desperate
And I didn't see it coming...

Young entertainer of the year, gold
Yes I felt golden for that moment I didn't believe the speech you gave
She sounded magical, she sounded perfect
That was the last gift you gave me
Before you stripped it all away.

The spotlight scared me and I froze
You scooped me up and the curtain went down
"You're gonna be a star" he whispers before he kisses me on the lips
And shoves his tongue down my throat

I bite hard and he drops me
But I knew no one was around
And you stripped what was left away.

Storing that story away I carry on full of shame
But my body feels different, blocked
I start to crave sugar and hate myself
Food becomes a refuge, my comfort blanket against the world
So I dive under the duvet and stay there
Hiding, denying, numbing, what he'd stripped away.

I'm sixteen now and this guy appears
He's intense and clever and fascinated with me
"I won't tell you I love you so that I can fuck you", he confesses one night.
I'm hurt but can't summon the courage to ask him to leave.
So we carry on as if somehow it's ok
And I fall into what I thought was love with him
What I thought was love

He breaks me open and after a year I let go
We get close and he's become my world
And I've become his
Inseparable we get the Romeo Juliet status
And then I realise that if I don't get out I will be in prison

So I end it
End what I thought was love.

He won't let go and loses the plot
I can't stand the guilt and numb out
Then he finds me one night and takes what's "his"
He strips what's left of me away.

As he leaves me he reminds me that he was my first
"You'll never forget me because I took your innocence"
As I lie there bleeding I shout
"You haven't taken anything!"
But I knew he had, I felt ripped and stripped away.

I'm a little older now and know there are
no victims, no villains
This time he's a French Lord
Prince and princess
Bastard and bitch
Wizard and witch
No ones gonna strip me away.

We're good lovers for years
But there's this divine delicate line

Between playing with our energy and crossing the line
But he does and I know
That in time, he will strip it all away.

SKELETON FRIEND

Doe eyed, vacant, I scan, I float...
A ghost riding freak way beyond a hunger strike
Beyond help, heat, heart...
Am I past all point of return so young?
How did this take over and strip me of soul
Wrenched from all homeostasis and sanity
Plunged into a cell that the external world see's as self-imposed....

It's behind these bars that I'm supposed to heal
Behind these doors that these "normal" doctors and nurses psychiatrists and
therapists
stare at me, a heap of bones
My skeleton friend has seduced my soul
and now this limbo is hard to trade in

This limbo stopped all the pain

this limbo was once such a gift to opt out
the ultimate universal anaesthetic
from the heavens sent until it took me past
the point of no return

I loved her
My skeleton friend
But I have to say goodbye now
Don't know how to unravel this knot
this 'habit', this ghost life...
Closer to the light,
just a bit more,
then you'll be all right,
my heart is sore,
but I must fight,
cold to the core,
I deny the night.

Lights blind my mind,
a piece of a damaged soul,
I let life fall behind.
Let my heart on parole,
but it's eternally blind,
an empty wound in my whole

peace I will never find...
Until I learn how to be kind
How to let go
How to unravel the grip of my
powerful queen of death
My Skeleton Friend...
and retrieve my soul.

SHY GUYS

The rugby player
directly opposites
got the big time yang thang
He's gorgeous and broad
with rock solid muscles
and a beautiful smile,
He's chatting me up at the bar
and it's fun
He's got the stereotypical x-factor:
that makes em alpha-hot status boosters
He's got a lot...
He's got the power
and a shower of fans
all around suckin him up
drowning him in ego boosting,
mood swinging,
uplifting confirmation

that he's a hot tot.
And he is!
But I'd never go back with him:
he's not a shy guy.

I'm approached by a "star"
and he's all a glowing at a
high profile gathering
You can smell the money
and power games all around
He's the hunter, I'm the pray
Reminds me of Hollywood days
shaking legs calmed
by champagne on tap
— the cruising around
and holding your own
on foreign ground

But this 'star's' so fucked
I can barely engage
He's a mess
a king baby supremo
dependant on self-reflexive glory
No real mojo

and a mother fucker no no!
I'd never go back with him:
he's not a shy guy.

My inbox is full
of strange stalky emails
from afar
this guy's a lady magnet
an emotional geographical "artist"
of the highest rank.
He's so pretty it's wrong
so engaging it's strange
his wall is a shrine
and so "after the chase"!
it's clear that it's a meet or delete stale mate...
but I can't even be bothered to take it seriously
'cos FB's a candy shop full of cyber games
'a projective identification inter-relation haven'
for the intimacy phobes —
and lost boys and girls so no reply it is.

I'd never give my energy to him: he's not a shy guy.
He taps me on the boat
and nervously asks for a light

I don't have one but catch his smile
His gaze can't meet mine
So sweet, so divine
He scuttles off and grabs his bags
His eyes are blue and open
an "unassuming Englishman" —
with repressed habits.
So he has my attention, he's got it.
He's a shy guy.

TOXIC REFLUX

Not too much
Hold that breath
Suck it in
Don't say that
Tip toe round
Never go there
Let that fester
Choke back those howls
Cloak that rage
Shut that mouth
Hold in those tears
Suck back that yell
Cage those fears
Hide that smile
Contract that belly
Cover those wounds

Control your intake
Expand your outtake
Consume that promise
Lie to yourself
Hide that power
Blame someone
Start it tomorrow
Churn in the night
Turn out your light
Toxic reflux culture

WOMAN IN THE MIRROR

I'm wondering what would occur
If a woman really saw herself in the mirror
A reflection that encompassed our divinity and individuality
Not an infection inflicted by patriarchal insanity
An infection that splits, fragments and scatters our sense of self
An infection that patriarchy imposed to keep us in competition.

United, we women would have a ball
United, we women could change what's in store
United, divine female power would mean so much more.

I'm considering then the power of a paradigm shift
And how that might be
A collective, reflective
Shift - from 3 to 4D.
A shift that could propel

A graceful step toward real harmony
I'm exploring the possibility that if a woman could see — really, really see —
her true nature, divinity, power and fragility
a shift could occur and stop the powers that be.
I understand how we got to this point
I understand how the pendulum has swung
And how and why it all begun
But enough's enough what's done is done.

We women have been fighting —
Fighting for so long.
Now I realise we had to reclaim, unravel and be reborn
But we women are women
Woman is divine
Not Barbies or Supermums
Or multi-tasking machines "prime time!"

See, the dichotomies just gotta go
It's so passé; it's such a "NO SHOW"
You can't be present when you're in your divided self
You can't be present in this madness; it's simply a "NO NO"
You can't step into self compassion or true equality
When you're competing with the other women and diminishing your own experience
and reality.

I'm so bored of blaming the "Yang gang"
Or mimicking them badly
I'm so bored of hearing women moan about man and his reality
And if a woman could really see herself in a mirror as she truly is
I wonder if she would drop her version
Of lack and imperfection
And embrace her immensity — change her reality?

'Cos this version's perverse
And I'm bored to death
Of this pantomimic gestalt that's so stuck
And time's running out!
If we women united then men could adjust
If we women united we would learn how to trust
If we women united our "Post Feminist" lust
Would subside and reside and transform into dust!
Now that process's gotta happen — Dust, ashes, compost...
It's an absolute must!
See, this environmental crisis that's killing us all
Is no more than an illusion invested in keeping us small.
We don't see our reflection in the mirror
We see our worst fears
'Cos this environmental crisis that values
"Barbie beauty, emancipation, and romantic

co-dependent tears" –
It's simply a cultural curse!

Now there's a chance it could change –
If we saw who we were and embraced the view.
Now there's a chance it could change –
If we saw who we were who we are,
Who we are and could be...

The woman in the mirror could change the world – the woman in the mirror is the
key to unfold –
That woman in the mirror could take hold –
If she came to life and death and universal gold.

And I'm praying she does it in time
'Cos the recapitulation process's just so divine!
To be reborn and create a new state
A "transgressive new Earth" –
Now that's just what she's calling for us all to give birth...

A DIFFERENT SECRET

There's a secret inside us all
that's unrelated to our story or glory
This secret isn't an energetic manipulation of an "American Dream"
or a linear version or narrative
It's no fairytale invested in "Happy Ever Afters"
or any kind of possession

There's an alchemic core inside us all
that binds every DNA molecule
and moment of love that's never lost or defined

There's an alchemic core that stores it all
and filters anything the alchemist chooses
to let go of, regenerate, embrace

There's potential for a whole new system to be born
Where energy is utilised differently, with love and equality
There's potential for a whole new world to deliver itself if Mother Earth hasn't
already had enough of our collective crap
There's potential for a whole new system to be born inside ourselves at any given
moment
To awaken and embrace our complete fragility and majesty

There's a mundane magic that's nothing to do
with our yoga practice, therapy sessions, Vipassana or raw food diet

There's a mundane magic that shines
through the simplest moments
There's a mundane magic that occurs
in every exchange
An ordinary, extraordinary magic

There's an opportunity to stop this collective imbalance
and redress things before nature wipes us out and takes over
There's an opportunity to wake up
and step out of our cultural coma
There's an opportunity to stop listening and playing out our lives
on autopilot and start hearing and acting as our magnificent selves

Ella Kate Reeves

Apocalypse please, this uncivilised state needs redressal
and it will be redressed like it or not
Apocalypse please, this society is sick
Apocalypse please, there's not enough humility
and collective consciousness to shift
Apocalypse please, I'm on my knees

MIND THE GAP

I've been weaved
From pieces of paper
More numerous than the leaves on the trees
They were made from.
I am the gap in the market
The letter crumpled
That told him why she couldn't stay
Or had to go
Either way he would never know
She'd left to fall out of urban madness
And into wild sanity.
Unravelling free.
That's me. The inbetweener.
I'm yesterday's obituaries.
I'm the fragmented dreams

Ella Kate Reeves

Of a thousand trees
That aspired to great heights
Projected through photosynthesis
I am water made solid
The register of your lives
from the most angelic to the most squalid.

DANCING THE DANCE OF BITTER SWEET

FA

Every mother's nightmare
Wasn't expecting you
Launched into a new zone
Zone unknown
A world where time
Took on a new line...
Quantum flow
Without any narrative
Any linear sobriety
A bittersweet prelude
On the medicine wheel
I had died and you arrived
Louis —- "Spiritual Warrior"

My sunshine — my reason for living
Knew something was wrong
Friedreich's Ataxia.
Bitter Sweet FA
Will slowly take your son away
Bit by bit you'll watch him die
No point in asking why
Life just isn't fair
"We all die Kate":
"Try to stay positive, maybe pray?"
But I fell apart
Into the abyss...
That only mothers
Who have lost children know
Unless they resist.
It's not pretty
I didn't want to die
Alongside this diagnosis;
This death sentence
I tumbled down
Into this terrifying place
Relentless, sleepless nights
Filled with nightmares from hell
No words, no life force...

Months and years
Of choking back tears and howls
Like an animal being slaughtered
Slowly, cruelly —
This grief cannot be spoken
It has a life and death of its own
So I'm surrendered to its rhythm
And it's a rhythm unknown.

PHOENIX FEVER

Quan Yin riding the dragon through chaos
to where she stands naked in the shower
holy and in heat
rubbing her body on Jesus
squeezing mango on her cheeks.
Belly him in oneness
Belly men in forgiveness

Guide me Gandhi with courage
through this strange evolution
of political pollution.
Organs have earthquakes underneath this skin.
You feel me Za Zen— so good—so good
Sacred whore, Mon amour,
Pele is stirring her magma core.
Dip your fingers in her melting pot if you dare.

If they enter in honor she lets them stay,
If not, she burns them to the bone.
When will man stop trying to own woman?
Forget your father and come with me
and create this travelling curiosity —
Sticky musk metamorphosis,
Bossa nova hips,
Put your lips to the chalice
spilling over with juices.
I need living water.
Daughters of Zion rising existence,
Dead Sea Scrolls.
Comb energy in my hair,
Tickle your breath up my spinal fluid
Vibrate my Goddess spot primal call.
Growing thrusts pulsing, pulsing thrusts motion.
Flamenco music rise
like the phoenix between my thighs.
We dream it.

Resonance flying believers.
Sushumna wave.
Dakini eyes.

Gospel revelations.
Sappho Island.
Murasaki Imperial.
Cypress waterfalls.
Whisper to me the stories
of the Heian Court of Japan
where sex was once sacred.
Touch me underneath.
Follow me into the dark.
Lick this wide Hecates Cave.
Wet dripping cunt.
King David cock.
Slide your jade stalk
down this deep pleasure valley.
Singing the heart open,
Singing all of her seasons awake,
Singing the world back into balance.
Let the rain have her way with us,
dripping wings,
as we weave ecstatic touch
our earth carnival.

I DO

I do
love you deeply
I do
love your heart and struggle
with it all
with life
with me
with you and I
I do
mean everything and none
of what I'm saying to you
I do
know why you are drawn to me
and want to reach out and wipe old tears from your eyes.
Kiss away the neglect and upset
I do

I do
love that you got down on one knee
and I said yes
I love your dreams and fantasies
sometimes, sometimes I join in
and say "I do"

I do
not know how to go from the depths of
our raw, free, gentle love
into a contract
a fish tank full of
other's trajections and ancestral knots
I do
not want to be tamed so that I
maimed, blamed and shamed
I do
not want to fall into
a death us do part trap
I do
not ever want to play that part
I do
dance between open and shut doors
that lead me to this edge

time and time again
I do
not want to stop feeling the potential
union and way it could be
if our "do's" met
I do wish that

and I do know that they haven't
so far, so far...
I haven't managed to say "I do"
but maybe someday...

RAG DOLL RESURRECTION

She knew pain of the physical kind —
she knew her threshold was high
comforted by the knowledge she'd survived
13 general anesthetics and near-death experience
an emergency caesarean, HELLP syndrome (a sure killer)
cancer of the cervix, 3 kidneys, and the diagnosis of her son "terminal"...
she almost thought she knew it couldn't be worse.
It couldn't be worse?
She wasn't sure what to do with herself after they told her?
What to do with her after the phone rings...
and someone says "*It's ok, we didn't find what we were looking for but...*
BUT.
BUT...you have this tumor...
there's no way to make the word tumor ok
It's 1mm from your optic nerve, deep in your brain"

and her ability to digest the blow
wore thin as time became "of the essence"
"THE ESSENCE"
Her essence was unusual to say the least
But surely that would work for her under this "duress"?
She knew she may not make it
She said her goodbyes and allowed wild cries
to flow and blow people apart those around her
"her soul" — which despite the odds and God's "divine un-laws",
tried to digest this and take it in her stride
take it in
her stride
this "beyond-challenging" ride
that seemed so surreal
she didn't have time to "come to terms" with...
or conceive or the unconceivable "reality"
that presented itself to her yet again
YET AGAIN — THE INCONCEIVABLE PRESENTED ITSELF
This nightmare became her reality
SO WHAT YOU GONNA DO WITH THAT?
It's what's happening
Here and now
Here and now
This is what life's dishing you out, girl

so ride it...ride it
and so she did
and she blew herself away...

PRACTICING FOR WHAT?

Funny how we "practice"
"Spiritual paths"
Get tied in knots
Idea's ideals
and fixed beliefs
All that orthodox crap
Those toxic hippycrites
and flakey drips
The "trustafarians"
Floating broken-hearted souls
Raw food airians.
Where's the breath
Being received
In the darkest hour?
The painless seat
in the tightest knot
The crux of asana.

Bored of acrobats
and ego-battles
Wrapped in spiritual frills
All the cloaked sticky mantras.
Practicing for what I ask?
It's the ones you cross
when the soul runs dry.
The ones you meet
in the roughest storms
The souls that
guide you back
to your deepest dream.
The alchemist in you
needs reminding —
to displace "the victim"
of your story
grace your own system
so don't fall victim
to a toxic rhythm —
To stand at the feet of your life
and use everything as fuel —
Lessons are blessings
blessings are lessons
and let your heart break.

The HEART can filter anything
that the alchemist embraces
and if you are awake
the heart will
break and break...

DISPLACING THE PRIESTESS

This 'she' is not pretty nor passive.

Or simply sexualised energy.

This 'she' is neither this .

Nor that.

And this 'she-wolf' knows...

That's there's far more

To everything than meets the eye;

This she is neither he nor she.

'She' is so fragile she could shatter

At any given moment.

So wondrous, she can seduce the moon and stars.

So powerful she blows everything apart.

This she is a million and more energies

Rolled into ether.

Neither this, nor that.

'She' is divine.

But far more than that;

This 'she' is in human skin and humility.
The key to she-wolf's aliveness...
Is silk-skin-wild-tender-fluidly
Rolled into a LIONS HEART.
'Divine', yes,;
but more powerful is
HER HUMANITY.

BETWEEN THE LINES

I will read
between your lines
and shit on your illusions
All those caramel-coated
systems that ripple
through your veins

I'm the empty shell
to the hermit crab
The black box
to the plane crash
The warm sake
to your raw fish
The dark night
to the lightening flash
You're the middle class digit prayer

to the one true God
You're the failed contraceptive
to my fertile womb
You're the smoker's cough
to the Marlboro man
I'm the hidden grass snake to
the unmade bed
You're the beefsteak fungus
to my hot hungry day
The too late apology
to the already said
I will read between
our lines.

EIGHT LASHES

I am a flirt of white
in the cave of the raven
the quiver waits for the birth burst
of the sun
I am a tease of roots nudging the rocks trying to budge the permafrost
I'm a flutter of eight lashes round a yellow eye that winks at the sky as I seize my one
brief chance to bloom and now I am taken by the shaman,
mixed with milkvetch, birch, moss campion
to make petalflesh limbstamen womb.
I am the wife of Ilukaq.

I stew berries and blubber for him to eat.
I chew sealskin to make soft boots for his feet.
With snow goose feathers, I sweep clean our home.
I carve him totems from the ice-bear's thigh-bone.
But oh I am another man's lover,

a man whose touch uncovers my desire
like a caribou licking up lichen from under the snow.

So what am I to do but harpoon Ilukaq,
leaving him frozen in the only pose he knows
—kissing the lip of the seal's breathing hole and
now I am snatched by the shaman
face smashed flat against ice shoulder blades
scolded into wings toes crooked into claws
voice scraped hoarse I hunt rodent dreams,
plunder the tundra, feed them to children,
stoke their troubled sleep

I am the famine-owl, a hunger-howl —the weeping of the people is steepled on my
wings
I'm the mood-most-foul of those who fail to claim the Pole — I'm so mad I could
wring my own neck
I am the sadness of the melt —my feather flecks reflect the eruptions of rock
through ice when I shut my sundog eyes
I'm shocked to realise that I'm still here

SHE-WOLVES IN SHELLS

Wolves in shells are crueler

than those left to run wild

Misanthropic mystic isn't something to be ashamed of untamed lunar queen

of the night skies shines

brightly over ecosystems rippling

through our veins and landscapes

deep down all around.

Caged she cannot roam or rule.

But wolves in shells bite back

rip and shred things apart.

She-wolf take it back.

PARADOXICAL UNION

From such aliveness — to death.

Navigating the realms

6th, 7th and 8th senses I'm thrown!

The shamans touch reaches my heart.

And, through WE journey far

Beginning the unraveling from the very start.

'Recapitulation' — to effulgence.

...I become light made solid

The register of all life's energies

From the most angelic to the most squalid.

Shakable, breakable, fragile

But FREE!

Who am I?

Life keeps showing me.

I'm eternally ME.

HONEYSUCKLE

I forgot how it feels to melt with a man
to press fiercely, intensely unrepentantly
until I opened up
my eyes from between his thighs
and felt his sighs in my mouth
south of his lips
I forgot the defined line of man-hips

I forgot how a man could make me feel
real unbreakable, yet sensitive shakable in the wet core of me impossibly
sweet circles sending me relentlessly higher
I forgot a man's fire

I forgot how to be led by a man
I took my chance and danced myself across him, up him — breathed him, licked and
grazed across his memories kissed their importance

I forgot the power of a man's glance
I forgot the woman I could be until he made me see my softly sensitive skin slipping
and sliding across him showed me how to make him feel like a man and set myself
free
I forgot how much fun a man could be

I love how he reminds me —
Honeysuckle bliss

PAN ETRATED

He is not the goddess; he is not the earth,
but he knows her with such delight.
His heart holds every leaf on every tree.
A doorway of spider silk and dirt opened.
His voice nudged my consciousness, there, and there,
Knowing where I could go that I hadn't been yet.
Always the playful voice led me on, pointed out the scenery,
The lichen on a rock, the purple mushroom.

His words dropped down my spine like a waterfall making music
As they fell through the suddenly open places,
Filling the echoing empty spaces in me,
The calcified fear and hopelessness.
Air brush splattered blood on deep blue,
Ripped and bleeding for nearly fifty years, could it finally clot?
His hands nudged the blood back in, healing the broken jar.

To wander the woods and find him suddenly there,
In a ring of trees,
Took my breath away
If he could be the god Pan,
What could I be?

WATERING MY SOUL

Just take it all
you've stripped my soul
"Relentless teacher"
My closest friends are gone
My son's on borrowed time
And my life's treadin' a fine line.
So take it all.

I've shed so many layers
Hit the floor again
and again and again...
Searched deep within and without 'til I'm left wandering woods and wild places,
praying on my hands and knees
in churches miles from anywhere
to try to understand, to let it all in...
and allow it just to be, to be

to reside and somehow settle in my soul.
You took it all.

You took my life
and gave me back a new view
A new perception and with it came
a responsibility so great—so great
How could I possibly have known how to live in that state?
"Died and returned"...so I burned and burned
So I disappeared into the ether
of alchemic darkness and wonder
You took it all...
I guess it simply was never mine to have.
Moment to moment —everything and nothing —
What an exquisite tango!
But this rhythm isn't mine
and these steps don't get taught or learned.
Surrendering to the void, the darkness...
sorrow that appears to engulf
every particle and wipe out all spirit, all carefreeness
all youth, juice and spontaneity

But there's a majesty in the darkness.
It burns all the edges away

and softens it all
and as I hit the floor again—
I'm different every time.
So take it. Nothing's here to stay.

So keep taking it away
and if nothing's really here to stay
at least I'm fluid now, not fixed.
And this disillusioned heap of broken-hearted stories
and fragility does know surrender
so very well now.
My God I used to love life so differently –
through the eyes of an ignorant child.
...so thank you for taking it all away.

I'M NOT JUST WRITING

I'm not just writing
I'm unearthing creatures inside
I tried to hide
And couldn't
Ancestral knots —
Hangovers from centuries ago
I'm not just writing
I'm unraveling my soul strung mojo.
Yeah — I need to reach deep in there!
And there
To fish out the crap
That's trapped and stale –
The calcified fear
All that loneliness
That got stuck in the web
Way, way back.
I'm not just writing

I'm reclaiming the witch and crone
Shedding down to bone
Climbing out of the closet
Redefining, refining
New skins and tails
Striking a chord in the spaces and gaps
Displaced by the confused parts
That got abused — raped.
I'm not just writing
I'm dancing into myself
Time and time again
Setting myself on fire
And free
I'm not just writing
I'm showing all of me.

ABOUT THE AUTHOR

Ella Kate Reeves was born in Brighton, UK.
She grew up in Horsham West Sussex and trained as a
dancer alongside her studies.

Although Ella is severely dyslexic she studied Media and
cultural studies and graduated from the University of
Sussex in 1999.

She went on to train as a Dance and Movement therapist,
psychotherapist and yoga teacher and now lives with her
son Louis who suffers from Friedreichs Ataxia (a rare
degenerative and life shortening genetic disease).

TESTIMONIALS

Anne Geragthy
(Author)

"Kate's poetry is not only original and beautiful it is challenging and visionary. Her poems take us into her journey and, as we read them, her struggles and surrenders become ours. She takes us with her into unfamiliar terrain, where her words themselves become elements of a living landscape. And Kate's journey is neither mundane nor predictable. She is living with challenges and demands that would floor many of us, yet she manages to transmute pain and loss into mystery and wonder. Kate's poetry performs the great alchemical transformation - from the chaos of human suffering into the creation of beauty, love, truth and a wisdom that knows there is something greater than pain and struggle, greater even than death. And this is the true beauty of her poetry. It shines with a light we all need. Thank you Kate - keep writing!"

Miranda Jay
(Psychotherapist, Musician)

"Gritty. Real. Raw. Potent. Ella Kate Reeve's poetry merges her lived reality with divinity, catalyzing our own awakening. An alchemist of our times extracting the soulful essence of truth, she casts her irons in the fires and we feel the heat as her words burn away. Her poetry is alive and lucid, a kind of Plutonic medicine that dances into our soul; an intimate waltz with death, loss, transformation and rebirth. Her poems should carry a warning label:
Read at your own risk."

Lisa Lovebucket
(Author)

"'Ella Kate Reeves is a new archetype: the kind of human being we need at the forefront if we are to weather the oncoming storm and come out thriving when the sun shines down on us once again. Kate can burn up the pain of the world in her little finger; envelop and annul it with her words; beguile and disperse it with her dance. Like a phoenix rising through an ice storm, she shines her light and warmth all around, melting hearts and inspiring minds as she soars ever upwards. Her every action abounds with the beauty and grace with which she conquers suffering and hardship, overcoming personal trials and adversity, and leading us all back to the light: a majestic homecoming 'indeed."

Ross James Brown
(Dancer, Poet)

"Your words directly connect me to the place I feel whole, complete, breaking through layers and layers of deep truth, taking me on little internal journey, powerful, so inspiring, gifted soul!"

Joe Hoare
(Psychotherapist)

"Ella's poetry is not for the faint-hearted, the pretenders, the sheen & gloss brigade, and 'look-but-don't-feel'. This is raw, real stuff and it rips the soul in agonising ecstasy. Please keep writing."

Wanda Ponder
(Life coach/Yoga teacher)

"Your poetry just leaves me reeling, dumbstruck, not sure what I'm feeling, your heart and soul bared to the world revealing, your inner truth, no concealing, and your words filled with so much magic and healing..."

Lightning Source UK Ltd.
Milton Keynes UK
UKOW03f0842210314

228583UK00001B/6/P